# HYACINTH E. GOODEN-BAILEY, M.A.

# POWER IN

# PRAYING

# THROUGH

## 52

## INSPIRATION NOTES

## BIBLE QUOTES

## PRAYERS

# ACCLAIM

*One of the most important tasks that we have as mothers and fathers is to pray over our children. We are to ask for God to protect them, guide them, and most importantly live in their hearts.* **Follow the wisdom of the author, Hyacinth Gooden-Bailey, to become comfortable praying and to 'cover' your children and loved ones with prayer each, and every day.** Faye Wilson, Ed. D., President, Salisbury District United Methodist Women & Minister of Music & Arts, Mt. Zion UMC (Quantico, MD) – Director, GeeFaye Associates_____

*Not too long ago, I lost my son, which ripped me apart. I didn't know how I was going to get through each day. Then, less than a year later, I lost two sisters five weeks apart. My faith in God never wavered, and this book tells us, that when we have suffered great loss, trust in God and pray for strength to go on. It tells us that prayers don't have to be long, but to the point. I keep this in mind when I pray at night.* **I will never lose faith in God, even when things don't happen right away after I pray, because God knows our needs, and when we need them. Therefore, this book should be read by everyone seeking comfort.** Kathy Huggins, Poet- Grace UMC, St. Albans, Queens, New York_____

*These readings are the epitome of a daily guidance, teaching us how to pray, why we should pray and how we can pray for whatever circumstances with which we are faced. The author shows* **succinctly that the true value of prayer is its influence in our daily lives, from early childhood to adult life. She points out correctly that it must not, however, be a wish list to the Almighty God. We must learn how to ask God to strengthen us and make our lives fulfilled in Him.**
Dawn Edwards-Raynold, M.Ed., NJ_____

# FOREWORD

Through 52 God-inspired Notes, 52 well-selected Bible Quotes and 52 very focused Prayers, intended to represent 52 weeks of any given year, the author provides very timely and pointed revelations about the power of praying about everything.

The dimensions and effectiveness of a prayerful life are unfolded bit by bit, as she gently guides those who have not indulged in prayer, as well as encourages those who might be getting weary. The reader realizes quickly that they have been missing something in their spiritual life, and begins to see how praying fits into different aspects of their lives.

No type of challenge is left untouched in this text. The social, psychological, emotional, professional and global are all laid out, exciting the reader to think, and get on board with praying.

The author emphasizes the amazing accessibility of God to everyone, and in every situation, providing specific Bible Quotes to support this truth. The supernatural Grace, Mercy, and Love of God are the key offerings laid bare.

# COPYRIGHT

# DEDICATION

**This book is dedicated to my late husband, Barrington, my children Marlon, Bridgitte, Raquel and Candace and my grandchildren present, and future**

Ezra 9: 5

"Then, at the evening sacrifice, I rose from my self-abasement, with my tunic and cloak torn, and fell on my knees with my hands spread out to the Lord my God and prayed."

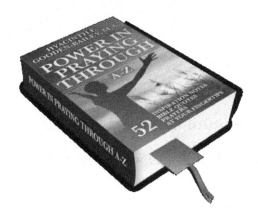

# HYACINTH E. GOODEN-BAILEY, M.A.

# POWER IN PRAYING

# THROUGH

**52 prayers, from A-Z**, to connect with the God of Glory during times of pain and times of celebration – hourly, daily, weekly and as often as necessary. Be specific when you pray. Learn to tell God what is bothering you and what you desire.

---

**Contact the Author: www.sapiencecoaching.com**

**Email: coachmenow@sapiencecoaching.com**

# TABLE OF CONTENTS

**PAGE**

# INTRODUCTION

*In this text, Quotes from the Bible are from the NIV (New International Version) translation.*

"As for me, I will call upon God; and the Lord shall save me. Evening, and morning, and at noon, will I pray, and cry aloud: and He shall hear my voice," (**Psalm 55:16-17**)

Learning to PRAY THROUGH is one of the most powerful skills that you could develop for the duration of your life. This book has been on my mind for years, but I kept shifting to some other topic and some other activity. However, the Holy Spirit is telling me that there are tons of people out there waiting to have it, so I need to get it done now. I trust that you are blessed by the quotes, the words and the prayers and that together they really energize you for 52 weeks. There are enough to take you through a calendar year, one prayer a week (52), a day, or all prayers every day, as you need them. You insert exactly what you need to connect powerfully with God, regarding your needs, desires and praises. I might need the prayer for health this week, while you might need the prayer for your finances and your fears. It's a smorgasbord of thoughts, the Word and prayer, to show you the freedom with which you may approach the throne of Grace, and to provide the confirmation that you will be heard. *'While we are yet asking, he will answer'*. What more assurances do you need? **We don't need a plan to pray, just pray. The important thing is to learn how to be in the right state of mind and the right condition of heart to receive.**

What 'praying through' involves are the following. Firstly, it's the idea that there should not be any season when we do not pray. We should pray through all the seasons of the year and the seasons of our lives. Secondly, we should remember to pray through each challenge until we see or experience the victory, that is, see our way beyond it. Next, that we face everything with the mindset that we are not giving up and that the end is on our lips. Our words confirm or deny our blessings.

**The open secret to well-being is praying in faith. It has been proven over and over in our society and around the world that all prosperity and power, which is not grounded in the worship of God, is doomed for downfall. It's before our eyes, if only we would see.**

Have you dreamt of being in the throes of prayer while you slept? I have, while writing this book. That is better than waking up scared from a horror dream, with your heart beating out of your chest. Pray through your subconscious.

## Growing up praying

I learned the power of prayer from a very young age, like 8.  I acted in Christmas plays which were taped, back then, at the public library in Kingston, Jamaica. I wish that I could get my hands on that long reel which was played back to us, to see how I looked several decades ago. We were angels and shepherds and everything else, re-living the birth of Jesus. Between that and weekly Good News Bible classes held in the neighborhood and Sunday School on Sunday mornings, Bible Correspondence courses, and a father who quoted the Bible night and day to everyone who would listen, I got a clear grasp of the fact that God was always waiting to hear from me.

My close girlfriends and I used to meet on Sundays, while others went to the movies, to pray for ourselves, our loved ones and our future.  As a child, I became my own little evangelist, distributing Bible tracts outside my gate to passersby, slipping others into the desk of my classmates and inviting younger students in High School to join me at lunchtime for prayer. This was serious business up to University level. Only prayers of faith kept me on the overcoming path.  However, I did not know that prayer would not just be vital for God to help me study and pass exams, but also to endure long fearful nights and tiring days. Prayer takes you through dealing with the manic-depressive challenges of your spouse, through pennilessness, and through not knowing what to do next, among other unnerving events.

*Prayer precipitates results, but your prayers need to be energized by your vision as well as your faith.* When real life hits you like a bullet from a gun, then you will realize why you had been praying all along.  So many people across the world are being tormented by other people's ignorance and barbarity because they have no knowledge of the living God or know that they have access to Him. The wars we fight are not just with physical and chemical weaponry, which would leave most of us too scared even to pray, but also psychological, mental, and supernatural - from realms we do not understand. **Prayer is preparation. It sends spiritual forces ahead of you. Nevertheless, don't forget that the battle is the Lord's.**

# PURPOSEFUL PRAYER

**".... even God, who quickeneth the dead, and calleth those things which be not as though they were." Romans 4:17 (KJV)**

Calling things which 'be not' as though 'they were', should lead us further to ACTING AS IF.  I won't go into that now, but that is the power state for real purposeful prayer. We must learn how to see beyond what is in front of us, beyond what we are feeling and beyond what fears creep up on us. God sees things as done, while we doubt whether they will be done. That's a real hurdle to leap over.

I want to share three qualities of purposeful prayer, which I have determined from my listening to God and from my experience. To be brief, purposeful prayer:

1. *intends creative results*

2. *has a built-in divine purpose, and*

3. *presupposes readiness to receive*

God doesn't need your help to have a prayer answered, based on the limitlessness of His power, but He does want 'to bless the work of your hands', rather than just to dish out blessings at your command. God wants to create on earth what is already established in Heaven. How does He do that?  By working with us and through us. We are co-creating, not just sitting by and watching.

I have never liked to talk too much about purpose since, how do we really know God's purpose until we fully achieve it. While we are in the process, that is not fully clear. However, I do like to talk about being purposeful. Being purposeful is praying and believing with the goal of matching our actions and life to God's larger plan, for now and for the future – which is unknown to us. The divine purpose of what we do today may not be served, or become clear until we have passed on.

Being ready to receive is also essential. It's like the wise brides who were ready for the marriage feast. The readier we are, spiritually and mentally, the more rapid the outcome and manifestation.

*Purposeful prayer also includes praying for others,* both those with whose challenges we are familiar, as well as those far away whom we do not know – like those refugees on the African continent, in Syria, in Myanmar and those living under bridges in America. We should especially pray for the scores of missing and trafficked girls and boys, happening right in our midst. Job was blessed and had his turnaround, the Bible tells us, when he prayed for his friends. The reason: everyone is part of God's greater plan.

In my experience, prayer takes you from studying as a student in school, within view and in earshot of the rum bar, to lecturing PhD candidates in Vienna. It takes you from quiet beginnings to hectic involvement in matters of global significance. My prayers of faith have brought me from not being able to afford the rental of anywhere suitable for my family, to buying a two-family home, all within the same space of time and with the same resources, as if we had been transposed to another universe. *Time and space are indeed transcended through prayers of faith. That is why the outcomes are considered miracles.* Sometimes we do not realize that we are living through a miracle, because the prayer is so far-removed from the event. Many people have come from nothing, and from the backwoods of the world to fame, fortune and great intellect, not necessarily because of their own prayers but because of the prayers of their parents and grandparents – of which they might not even be aware. God is faithful, so He honors prayers, never leaving any unnoticed.

## Being in prayer is a lifestyle of power

You don't have to be holy to pray, but it certainly gives you the advantage if you are a saint who stays in the presence of God all the time. You may be Barabbas, hanging on the cross beside Jesus, and have your prayers heard. Prayer has more power when you use God's own words to fuel your praise and your supplication to Him. God likes that, and He acts more promptly when you use His Word in your prayer, so don't fail to add that to the prayer examples in this text, in addition to the specifics of what you are asking for. *Praying doesn't mean that you have no work to do.* It does mean, however, that you will not spend time and energy on misdirected actions and preoccupations.

**If you are a parent, you cannot stop lifting up your children to God. You must command the angels to surround them 24/7.** There is no other way to transcend the world we live in today. More importantly, pray with them, and let them learn early to pray for themselves. Let them hear that you love to talk to God and let them witness the results of prayer.

Prayer is not just words or repetition of words. When we pray, we do several things simultaneously. Among them are the following: we have our bodies healed without knowing that something is going wrong, we prophesy what we want to happen, we speak new situations into being, we clear the atmosphere, we produce new thoughts and ideas, we dis-assemble crookedness and blocks and make a way through the rubble and most of all, we are strengthened to move up and forward. We are warned that we spoil our prayer, if we 'ask amiss.' To ask amiss is to ask with the wrong motive, without faith or not according to God's will. That means that haphazard prayer will not be answered.  Please refer to the Word of God for guidance.

If you ever doubt whether you are praying right, recall the following:

"But let him ask in faith, nothing wavering. For he that wavereth is like a wave of the sea driven with the wind and tossed," (James 1:6). We should try to keep that image in mind.

**Prayer as first resort and continuous intervention**

*Our prayers are attached to our dreams. Our dreams are those things that wait at the windows of heaven to be opened for us.*

Prayer comes to the rescue all the time. It works mightily when done in advance of challenges, as well as instantly when delivered with boldness. You don't know how it's working or when, but it always does its job. You will see from the Bible verses – why. Prayer takes over when life brings negative surprises and it gives you the right energy to overcome when you don't know what to do – when a daughter gets pregnant too soon, when a son goes to jail, when a husband leaves for good, when a wife falls ill, when a child is defiant or refuses to go to school, when the bank account is zero, when the job disappears, when there is sudden death, and when disasters of all kinds hit. **Prayer can be counted on to help you make the right choices, and at the same time upholds you, when you**

**have made the wrong ones and must face the results.**
Never say: *the only thing left to do is pray.* That's
offensive to God. Rather, begin all processes with your
prayer of faith, so that even when you forget to believe,
your prayers will continue working.

One very important point about prayer is that it ought to
take place during a conversation with the Creator and is
not a one-sided lament. For prayer to be fully effective we
need to come to it, understanding that we should also
listen and be willing to obey. *Prayer is not making a phone
call and leaving a voicemail, and never expecting a call-
back or instructions.* Praying generates the unstoppable
feeling of the Presence. The mighty presence of God. **If
we hold on to that Presence then we are really in
uninterrupted prayer mode, whether we are awake or
asleep**. That's how we often wake up to solutions, after
going to bed, not having a clue.

**Praying any place, any time**

In these pages, I hope you will get excited about what the
Word of God promises and about the power of prayer.
You may use these prayers to get in the habit of praying
about everything but please SPEAK TO GOD ON A
PERSONAL LEVEL. Pray to God as the Spirit leads you, even
when stuttering, and inarticulate. It does not matter. The
Spirit is waiting to re-interpret your words so that your
prayers will go unhindered up to the Mercy Seat of God.
The Spirit understands everything about all requests from

everybody. God hears the prayers of those who are guilty and in prison, as well as those who are falsely accused and convicted. He hears the prayers of the suffering mothers and children all over the world on the streets, as well as the woman who just got divorced and is left penniless by her husband. He is just as ready to hear the prayer of those who want to be recognized and rewarded for their good work in the office or business and are being shortchanged. Bring it all to the throne. Walk your park with the Word of God on your cellphone and pray in words or song as you entertain God's presence in peace, calm and nature. That's a great habit to have, even if you don't jog. Talk about stress management? Here is a good beginning.

**The Praying Habit**

Praying is both a tool and a weapon, to be used wisely. Praying is simultaneously the humblest and the most powerful way to your well-being. Not reality TV, not 15 minutes of fame in media, and not the most expensive designer wear. God is never tired of hearing from us, so he will not say: Oh, you again? He invites us to call on him continuously. Preachers, don't use prayer to scold either sinners or believers. There is no barking and biting in prayer. There is confession. There is praise. There is thanksgiving. There is desire expressed and there is surrender to God's mercy and grace. That is why we keep praying.

When we pray we confirm the promises of God and make them the basis of our hopes and aspirations. Believers should run after each other to pray together, since the Bible tells us that God is partial to prayers agreed on by more than one person praying together. "Again, truly I tell you that if two of you on earth agree about anything they ask for, it will be done for them by my Father in heaven" Matthew 18:19

**At the church where I worship in Queens, New York**, our former Pastor started the congregation on a diet of daily prayer at 6 a.m. and noon, and for over 3 years a devout group of saints has been calling in and praying about specific issues arising, and studying the Bible for an hour. Sometimes the group was as large as 80. How wonderful that believers want to meet and pray and study when they could be sleeping. They do this on the way to work, or preparing breakfast or preparing for work. That habit obviously pays and will pay dividends yet unseen. Prayer produces fine gold.

Decade after decade, I have lived through God's handling of the impossible, which is His specialty. That does not mean that I get everything I want, or whenever I want it. However, do you want to tour the world, without getting in debt for it, pray. Want to enjoy true and enduring love, pray. Want to get back your health when the Doctors don't know what to do, pray. Want to get all your children the best education possible, pray. Worried about your children, at any age, pray. There is no situation which will ever be outside the purview of God's power, grace or love. We could go on and on. It's not a matter of asking for things, but of being so embedded in prayer and praise that what you can hardly imagine will walk right into your life, only because it is the Will of God. Prayer will take us repeatedly out of 'circumstances' and 'situations' to experience the *realm of the supernatural being practically ordinary to us,* as believers.

If you will allow me, *let me emphasize that it is a mockery to prayer to only pray and not act in accordance with what you are praying for.* Just as 'faith without works is dead', praying and doing nothing about what you are praying for is rather empty. If you pray for good health, then you should do things commensurate with good health; if you pray for wealth then don't go wasting money; if you want wisdom, don't spend time doing foolishness. It's pure logic. Of course, there are points at which you may have to 'Be still and know that I am God' when the Spirit tells you to do so.

**Jesus's model prayer, given to his disciples, provides the most effective structure for our prayers**. We praise and honor God, we clear our hearts and minds by asking for forgiveness, we thank our Father for all His goodness and then we beseech him for what we want to happen and then acknowledge His faithfulness, in that our prayers will be heard. If you gave up on praying, start again, and if you never really prayed in earnestness, begin to do so. *Prayer is super-telepathy. It speaks to all circumstances far and*

*near and it transcends all interferences to get to the*
*Source, so - above all - PRAY.*

**I have observed, as a Coach of personal re-invention,**
**that an increasing number of persons are realizing that**
**what they need is spiritual intervention, rather than**
**attempting fixes for social, stress-driven, relationship,**
**career or financial concerns. They are asking specifically**
**for 'spiritual counseling', but from what Source?**

Finally, I must add this. I want to quote Ecclesiastes 5:2:
*'Do not be quick with your mouth, do not be hasty in your*
*heart to utter anything before God. God is in heaven and*
*you are on earth, so **let your words be few**.'*  Just come to
the point purposefully, when you pray.

Here, in *Power in Praying Through*, you will find a prayer
to match most situations with which you might be faced
over the next 52 weeks of the year. Your year may begin
at any time. Take advantage of it and keep your focus.

# A

## AFFLICTION

Afflictions are like curses. They could also be doorways to greater things. They are unwanted, but they come, and when they come, they often come triple. Onlookers call it your punishment or your test, depending on their own outlook but it does not matter what others think, it is what you are going through that is important. *'Be joyful in hope, patient in affliction, faithful in prayer'.*

Afflictions can be addictions that you cannot shake, or anything you are doing or accepting which is sabotaging your present or your future. People can be our biggest affliction, creating uninvited burdens in our lives. Afflictions hurt and feel like they will never go away, especially when the afflicted feels weak, in the face of the experience. Let's take it to the Lord in prayer. See what the Word says next.

## Bible Verse:

The righteous person may have many troubles, but the Lord delivers him from them all; he protects all his bones, not one of them will be broken. **Psalm 34:19**

## Prayer:

*Almighty God, I cast my cares at your feet and ask you to give me more courage and faith to face my afflictions (and addictions) today. I speak to the evil that is attacking my life right now. I speak with the power of the blood and take authority over this distress which is trying to drain me of my life. In you, oh Lord, I live and breathe and have my being, so I reject this nuisance in my life and believe for full deliverance from this plague which is blocking me. In Jesus's name, Amen.*

# ATTITUDE

Our attitude towards God affects our attitude toward ourselves, toward others and toward life's ups and downs. Our attitude towards ourselves affects how we receive and treat others. Too much pride will lead to looking down on others or being so self-centered that we do not see the needs of others. An attitude of thankfulness and praise toward God leads to humility and caring for others. We can either be open or closed toward learning from others, depending on our attitude. We may even block God's guidance, if we think we know it all.

Attitude is picked up by observers even before we open our mouths or take any action. Children who come to school with a bad attitude that was not corrected at home, do not learn well or get along with other classmates and then that is taken to the workplace and even to the CEO's suite or to the leadership of a country, spilling over into the lives of others around them – wrecking a company or even a society.

## Bible Verse:

...put off your old self, which is being corrupted by its deceitful desires; to be made new in the attitude of your minds; and to put on the new self, created to be like God in true righteousness and holiness.  **Ephesians 4:22-23**

## Prayer:

*Great God of Heaven I bow before you today and ask that if there is an attitude in me, which actually sabotages my own success in different aspects of my life, if there is an attitude that I display which does not reflect Jesus, rid me of it now. Shine the light on me, Lord, and help me to change.  I surrender all my attitudes to you and ask only for that mindset and response to life and to my circumstances which reflect your wonderful grace, peace and power. In the name of Jesus, I pray. Amen.*

# B

## BEHAVIOR

People's behavior, in this century, has ceased to reflect any sense of shame or propriety. Public and business leaders and supervisors in different sectors display bad behavior unapologetically, unless of course, they are caught in the act – on audio or video – or may suffer some negative consequence. Behavior today is further influenced and controlled by the illicit drugs used by a large percentage of people round the clock, and not just for recreation.

It would help if people paused after an altercation or any exchange with another human and check if their behavior was offensive, or negative in its effect. Behaviors are remembered and do tarnish all future interaction with others, whether involved or observing. Children today don't seem to know what is acceptable behavior, whether public or private. They are unfortunately making up their own rules for behavior, not just with others but with their own parents. Parents are scared, these days, of their own offspring, long before they have finished middle school. The young are exposed to too many bad-behaving adults, both in the media and directly around them.

## Bible Verse:

But the fruit of the Spirit is love, joy, peace, patience, kindness, goodness, faithfulness, gentleness, self-control; against such things there is no law. **Galatian 5:22-23**

## Prayer:

*Sweet Lord and Savior, I ask for your full examination of my behavior at home with my family, with my friends, with strangers who upset me, with colleagues at work and with those in authority over me. I rely on your guidance, Lord, so that I do not offend and if I do, to make amends. Help me to refrain from any word, action or even thought, which would deny the wonderful love, grace and mercy you offer, my Lord.  In your precious name, I pray. Amen.*

# BELIEF

At the core of all our lifestyle and choices is the belief system by which we operate. Most times it's unconscious and never reckoned with by us. Often, we do not know what exactly we believe or how that belief influences what we think, or do. We inherit beliefs. We learn false ways of believing or re-interpret what we think we believe, to suit what we want out of life. As a Christian, your basic belief is that there is a God-head made up of the Father, the Son and the Holy Spirit and that the Son, Jesus Christ came and died thousands of years ago, precisely to save you from your eternal damnation.

Dig deeper to find out what your beliefs really are and how they form the source of your strength or weakness in coping with life. What you believe, you repeat in the words you speak, in the thoughts you think, in how you view others and interact with them.  Each time that you activate that belief system, you confirm that belief to yourself and make it more embedded in your being, no matter how false and irrational it may be.

## Bible Verse:

Beloved, do not believe every spirit, but test the spirits to see whether they are from God, for many false prophets have gone out into the world. **1 John 4:1**

## Prayer:

*Dear God, help me to understand more deeply what my faith in you really means for my life. Let me know, by the leading of the Holy Spirit, how you see me and how I should see myself. Guide my understanding of how I should worship and trust you. Let my life match my spiritual beliefs in every respect. Let me not leave you out of my daily activities and out of the goals that I set. Help me, Lord, to remember to turn to your Word for the final word on what is wrong and what is right, and lead me into your way of truth today. In Jesus's precious name, I pray. Amen.*

# C

## CREATIVITY

Some people appear more creative than others but all of us do apply creativity to our daily lives to manage new or trying situations. Creativity is a blessed ability to have. The more creative, the more income you may earn, and the more positive changes you can make in your life. Creativity allows you to move along rather than remain stuck indefinitely, whether on the job or in personal living. It also provides a happier state to be in, as you see more possibilities rather than more defeat, when faced with a challenge.

God's handiwork is the best canvas of creativity, from the stars and planets in the universe to the beautiful plants and flowers worldwide, the variety of uses of all created things and the diversity of people on the planet. We can look to this high Source of Creativity to master this skill repeatedly.

## Bible Verse:

And he has filled him with the Spirit of God, with wisdom, with understanding, with knowledge and with all kinds of skills – to make artistic designs for work in gold, silver and bronze, to cut and set stones, to work in wood and to engage in all kinds of artistic crafts.  **Exodus 35:31-33**

## Prayer:

*Dear Heavenly Father, as the Creator of the Universe, I know for sure that you are the unlimited source of creativity, to which I may turn at any time for direction and sustenance. I am stuck, Lord. I ask you to open the fountain of creativity so that I can come up with the right, bright ideas I need now. I need to come up with something unexpected, something unique, to get me over this hurdle. I pray for the clearing of my mind and thoughts so that a new, creative frame of mind can take over and produce results speedily. Let my mind, O Lord, be in your mind so that I overflow with great ideas and the skill to execute them. I thank you in advance as I receive what I ask for. Amen.*

# CONFUSION

Many people are walking around feeling confused, even though they give the impression that they have things under control. Confusion arises when we have too many choices or see no choice at all – where to live, when to move, what job to pursue, what to do about the children, what to do about the spouse, dealing with illness, how to handle financial woes and on and on it continues.

Not knowing whether to turn right or left at any given time, is not necessarily a sign of confusion. We all go through transitions. They are just points at which you are questioning, searching, adjusting and assessing. Real confusion is when you are in such a state that you choose what is not in your interest, because you have no clarity, and you trust others to decide for you, rather than trust yourself and your inner, spiritual guidance.

## Bible Verse:

For God is not a God of confusion but of peace.
**1 Corinthians 14:33**

## Prayer:

*Lord of Heaven, I humbly bow before you and seek your mercy as I try to sort through the confusion that I feel. Help me to see more clearly and get a revelation from your Holy Spirit. Lord, help me to relax in your care, knowing that I am under your wings and that I am wise enough to make the right move and that no matter the outcome, you are with me. I ask you to lift my spirit at this moment so that I can think in a more positive way and therefore see the solution which I know is waiting there for me to see. I praise and honor you, Lord, as I wait to have victory over my confusion. In your blessed name, I pray. Amen.*

# D

## DECISIONS

Whether we believe it or not, we are constantly making decisions – whether to stand still, sit down, walk, run, smile, frown, buy or sell, work or stay home, stay put or seek promotion. We are constantly forced to decide and even when we leave things to happen on their own, the outcome is still the result of a decision. Albeit, a decision to be indecisive. The important decision to surrender to Jesus Christ has life-long and eternal effects for each of us. Other decisions fall in line behind that one.

Let us continue to plant seeds of every kind, for God Himself will give the increase, so that others will come to make their own decisions to accept Christ as their Savior.

Exercise your power and faith by deciding for what will enhance your health, your peace-of-mind, your wealth and your personal growth and development. Learning decision-making skills is a very important asset in business and applies also to every single aspect of life.

## Bible Verse:

'Call to me and I will answer you.  I'll tell you marvelous and wondrous things that you could never figure out on your own.' **Jeremiah 33:3**

## Prayer:

*Dear Loving God, today I have a few important decisions to make and I ask you to whisper in my ears and assure me that no matter what, you will cover me and make my decision fruitful. I am afraid of making a big mistake, but I am aware that it is up to me to determine what I want. I know that you have plans for me to bless me, and so I ask for your guidance so that I stay in line with your will and purpose for me. I trust you this moment, and will step forward in agreement with your Holy Spirit, to achieve what is best for me and my family. In your precious name I pray. Amen.*

# DISAPPOINTMENTS

Disappointments are hard to deal with. They can only be ignored if you really don't care, and then they wouldn't really be disappointments, would they?  Disappointments are greater, when you have your mind completely set on certain outcomes or consider yourself fully deserving of something. Women are greatly disappointed when the men they love turn out to be horrible monsters, not living up to the calling of 'husband'.  Parents are highly disappointed when their offspring ignore all the careful upbringing and go their own wayward way.  Workers are disappointed when employers hold back promotions and salary increases or relieve them of their jobs.

Sometimes we are disappointed because we have false expectations. The world is full of disappointing scenarios from top to bottom, since we cannot match up our own personal expectations perfectly with the demands and schemes of others. It's only when we embrace the idea that *'all things work together for good'* that we can handle disappointing events in our lives.

## Bible Verse:

"For I know the plans I have for you," declares the LORD," plans to prosper you and not to harm you, plans to give you hope and a future." **Jeremiah 29:11**

## Prayer:

*Almighty Father, today I know that you – as the all-knowing God – can fully see how disappointed I am with how many times I have been passed over and how long I have been praying for a positive result to all my efforts. I am weary of waiting and am very angry at how much I must endure while others are receiving exactly what they want. Forgive me for being impatient but I can barely stand to continue as I am. Help me to deal with this feeling. Help me to remember that you have a higher purpose for everything that happens in my life. Help me to deal with this test. Please restore my joy and give me a new vision from which to proceed, as I wait on you. I call you Abba, Father, and give you praise. In Jesus's name. Amen.*

## EXCELLENCE

Aiming at excellence may be too stressful for some people, so they settle for the mediocre. That should not be you. Excellence should be the target for every action that you take. Aiming for the highest should be the norm in your life, to ensure that you remain in the realm of the best and not that of the least.

Excellence does not apply only to learning and academics, or to the workplace but to speech, communication, relationships, and all other aspects of body, mind and spirit. Doing excellently should be the hallmark of Christians since our Source is the author of everything great and mighty and inexplicable to the highest intellect.

**Consider yourself as someone who has both the right connections and the right implements to achieve excellence in every area of your life.**

## Bible Verse:

And this is my prayer: that your love may abound more and more in knowledge and depth of insight, so that you may be able to discern what is best and may be pure and blameless for the day of Christ, ... **Philippians 1:9-10**

## Prayer:

*Dear Lord and Master, I ask you to assist me in this project so that I will do it to the best of my ability. I am overloaded, but I really want this to be well done. I need your help to keep my focus. Let me be willing to receive the guidance which I know is available from the Holy Spirit, and the help that is available to me.*

*Guide me to the right sources of information so that I may produce at the level that will bring you glory and confirm that you are the source of my wisdom. I declare now that what I do is led by you, dear God, and that I am well able to achieve the highest and the best. These things I pray in no other name but your mighty one, Jesus. Amen.*

# ENCOURAGEMENT

Parents spend much of their time encouraging their children. If children only knew that beyond the food, clothes and shelter, encouragement was a key factor in allowing them to grow and become their full being. It develops self-esteem. Everyone needs encouragement when they fall and bruise their knees, when they spill the food, when they leave the house feeling that they are the worst-dressed, or fail in what they thought they had mastered. Beyond that, we should learn to encourage ourselves.

Managers need to encourage, not penalize, workers. Leaders need to encourage the people. Pastors need to encourage the saints – as much as rebuke or criticize them. Husbands need to encourage wives - even when they appear to be superwomen. Women need to encourage men who might be feeling emasculated. Encouragement is a salve for hurts and insecurities. Give it with meaningful, rather than flattering, words. Encouragement is even needed when you are doing well, because you may be second-guessing yourself. We should give encouragement and listen when we get it. Let's be encouraged above all by the Word of the Lord.

## Bible Verse:

I lift up my eyes to the mountains – where does my help come from? My help comes from the lord, the Maker of heaven and earth. He will not let your foot slip – he who watches over you will not slumber; ……. the LORD will watch over your coming and going both now and forevermore. **Psalm 121:1-8**

## Prayer:

*Most High God, I am about to give up. Do you see my tears? I am about to give up. It is all pointless. I am about to sit here and do nothing more. You know that I am weary. Speak to me, Lord. I am waiting. I know that this is a test of my faith. I have run out. I am waiting on you, Lord. Thank you that I have your promise of a better future than I can imagine. I am glad that your thoughts are not my thoughts. Dear Savior, I am believing that my answer is on the way, so I offer my prayers now, in accordance with your promises. Increase my faith. In the name of my loving Lord. Amen.*

# F

## FEAR

Fear is a constant factor in modern society. Fear of crime, fear of aging, fear of job loss, fear of financial lack and on and on it goes. Fear propels those who have no spiritual guidance, to act irrationally and cause acrimonious situations every way they turn. That fear even prevails between nations and regions at the Government level, threatening us with global war. Fear can eat at our soul and leave us living only by reaction and sinking deeper into inaction.  Fear of being without leads the thief to steal. Fear of not knowing leads the student to cheat. Fear of not being lovable leads people to connect with others who really don't love them.

Fear messes up our vision of what is possible and diminishes the drive to move toward what's best. In fear, all we see is what could go wrong and the worst that could happen. God's word assures us that *He has not given us the spirit of fear, but of love and of a sound mind.* Indeed, harboring fear for a long time, could drive you crazy, as when the domestic-abuse victim reacts lethally. False fears about many things do come to bitter ends.

## Bible Verse:

"Have I not commanded you? Be strong and courageous. Do not be afraid; do not be discouraged, for the LORD your God will be with you wherever you go." **Joshua 1:9**

## Prayer:

*Dear Lord and Master, as I bow before you today. I rejoice that I can live without fear. I rejoice that even when I am not sure what is around the corner, I can put aside fear and replace it with faith. I ask for the energy of faith to pervade my thoughts and feelings and that fear be a foreign word to me, no matter what. I ask you, Lord, to take this burden which is haunting me and help me replace it with trust, faith and praise. I denounce and walk away from any fearful sentiments and I receive rest and sweet sleep because I know that is what you want for me. These mercies I beg in the name of the blood of Jesus that has been shed for me. Amen.*

# FAMILY

Family is a word that applies to different social arrangements in this young century. The traditional family of father, mother and child has changed drastically to blended families of several mothers and several fathers and children of mixed parentage, alongside the traditional extended family of uncles, aunts, grandparents and cousins. The term 'family' is used to refer to criminal groups as well as church and other social groups, each with the basic meaning of sharing one culture, one approach to life and a mutual collection of resources.

Even in the best arranged families the worse things are increasingly happening. Abuses of all kinds abound. If you can't trust your family member, who can you trust? More pain and suffering sometimes occur inside a family rather than generated from outside. The reason is that the hurt runs deeper where one is expecting love, support and deep sharing and gets the opposite instead, or perceives the worse. Today, instead of spelling 'joy', family spells 'stress' and distress. Let's pray to turn that state around.

## Bible Verse:

But he said to me, "My grace is sufficient for you, for my power is made perfect in weakness." Therefore, I will boast all the more gladly about my weaknesses, so that Christ's power may rest on me...For when I am weak, then I am strong. **II Cor.12:9-10**

## Prayer:

*Sweet Jesus, maker of heaven and earth, I pray on behalf of all who struggle to form and maintain stable families in my neighborhood, in our country, and in the world at large. Rescue the poor children who live on the streets, without a loving family, vulnerable to abuse by preying strangers. Dear God, I invite your intervention in my own family and my children's family. Let those who are estranged return home to caring and forgiveness.*

*I ask you to arrest us when we are making the wrong moves, saying the wrong things, which will cause conflict and chaos. Lead us to love instead of bitterness. Help us to celebrate the blessing of loved ones and to build loving relationships with others. I pray this prayer trusting you fully to rescue us from ourselves. Amen.*

## THE LORD'S PRAYER  - MATTHEW 6, 9-13

After this manner therefore pray ye:

Our Father which art in heaven, Hallowed be thy name.

Thy kingdom come, Thy will be done in earth, as it is in heaven.

Give us this day our daily bread.

And forgive us our debts, as we forgive our debtors.

And lead us not into temptation, but deliver us from evil:

For thine is the kingdom, and the power, and the glory, for ever.

Amen.

**King James Version (KJV)**

# G

## GRATITUDE

Starting from a place of gratefulness is a great start for any undertaking. If you undertake any project or experience with the thought of how thankful you are to be part of it, to be qualified for it, to be given the opportunity, and that God is seeing you through it, you are definitely ahead of the game. How powerful it is to be engaging in something, being confident that the outcome will be great, only because you have already given thanks for what you are envisaging by faith. That is why when others win, it looks so unlikely, because they are probably doing what you have not done – by way of being in a state of 'gratitude'. Think that through and pray about it. Then learn to practice it. Give thanks. Your cup is running over.

Gratitude spills over into our charitable behavior and into the quality of service and attention to the needs of others, while others question the motivation. They call it 'giving back', but we are not giving back to people. We are giving back to the Source – God.

## Bible Verse:

Give thanks to the Lord, for he is good. His love endures forever. Give thanks to the God of gods. His love endures forever. Give thanks to the Lord of lords, His love endures forever" **Psalm 136:1-3**

## Prayer:

*Dear Father, we humbly ask for your forgiveness when we have not been grateful, when we have ignored the riches already bestowed on us. We thank you for life, for our bodies and all its incredible functions, for those who help us each day of our lives, for the plans you have to bless us, of which we have no idea. Lord, help me to thank you, rather than complain. I thank you, Lord, for my guilt-free life, because I have your salvation. I thank you for your Word which promises that I will be blessed and not cursed. I receive all your promises with all my heart, and praise your matchless name for your tender mercies. Only in Jesus's great name. Amen.*

# GOALS

A goal is a destination. Goals are also points along a path. When we set a goal, we often write it down (or fail to) or tell others, and we try to clear the way to have that goal happen. However, just stating a goal, as we have experienced, does not necessarily get us there. Sometimes, we are forced to reduce goals or increase them and that relates to both personal, professional and business goals.

We sometimes set goals and are disappointed because the time-frame we set for them was not met, not realizing we had a faulty deadline or too much goal to handle. That means that goals need to be carefully thought out and not haphazardly declared. Setting the goal alone does not make it happen. The other matter is that your goal should be your own and not someone else's that you joined - like 'let's lose 10lbs each'. The joint effort may not be equally correct for each person.

Notwithstanding, setting goals is important for everyone. If you are living without any goals in mind, or any goals working toward, you are merely floundering and will not get to anywhere special.

## Bible Verse:

"For the revelation awaits an appointed time; it speaks at the end and will not prove false. Though it lingers, wait for it; it will certainly come, and will not delay. **Habakkuk 2:3**

## Prayer:

*Lord and Master, help me make up my mind as to what goals I want to set in my life at this crucial time. I know that I should seek direction from you, because you are God and you know what is best for me, but how do I do that? Please show me. Help me see the cues. I am not sure if I am on the right track. Should I just stay in place and be happy with what I am doing and what I have, or should I really be aiming for more? Help me to sort out whether I have too many goals or if I am standing in my own way. Give me the energy and drive to pursue the goals which I do set so that I will be as successful as I want to be. Let my goals all honor your mighty name as I surrender my will to yours. I pray this prayer in Jesus's glorious name. Amen.*

# H

## HEALTH

Without good health, everything else suffers. However, people spend more time on external, unimportant matters rather than pursuing health matters. Health is largely a matter of internal management and inner thoughts. The mind and the body work together, as well as the mind, body and spirit, so health is not what pharmaceuticals the doctor prescribes to dull symptoms rather than to cure. Health begins – in my judgement – with thinking 'healing' all the time.

Thinking healing is to expect your body to behave the way God intended it to, repairing and replacing everything that needs attention, the same way that we change our skin continuously without even paying attention.

Unfortunately, with all the chemicals approved by health agencies and pumped into our daily foods, we are up against physical battles that God never intended us to fight. We are being slowly poisoned, and we even pay for it willingly. Without careful notice of what we consume, and without daily prayer, where does that leave us?

## Bible Verse:

"Worship the Lord your God, and his blessing will be on your food and water. I will take away sickness from among you, and none will miscarry or be barren in your land. I will give you a full life span." **Exodus 23:25**

## Prayer:

*Father, I lay my ailments before you because I know that 'by your stripes I am healed'. You are willing and ready to heal me of all my diseases. I refuse this interference in my health. I speak the Word now with authority and command this distress to go. I receive only health and wholeness in my being. I ask for guidance, O Lord, to keep eating right, exercising and resting to maintain my good health. I accept my cleansing right now and praise you for what you have promised me. I surrender to your healing power and am believing the resurrecting power of your Word and the blood of Jesus. I receive with joy. Amen.*

# HAPPINESS

What is happiness? It's what we feel when we are engaging in some activity, or we are in some environment, or we are looking at something, which is pleasant and enjoyable. We often make happiness our top goal. We work hard to make sure we secure future happiness. We marry intending to secure long-term happiness. We build a grand home expecting to be happy in it and we often think – I would be happy, if only I had, or if only I could do so and so. This quest for happiness is so illusory, and yet generations of humans have continued the quest.

Sudden changes in events and destiny rob us of happiness over and over. It's the 'joy of the Lord' that we really need. With the joy of the Lord, you can be in a sad situation and yet not lose that joy. It is aligned with the 'peace which passes understanding'. It's the state of happiness which does not shift and keeps building you up. That is why we must keep connected to the true and loving Source through prayer and loving worship.

## Bible Verse:

Take delight in the LORD, and he will give you the desires of your heart. **Psalm 37:4**

## Prayer:

*Father in heaven, thank you for the joy of my salvation. Thank you for filling me with your peace so that I can face every attack or loss with the assurance that what you wish for me is that I 'be in health and prosper even as my soul prospers'. I thank you for all your good favors in my life and I celebrate your goodness to me and my family. I know that there is overflow coming my way, so that I can praise you and be happy, without even seeing or being able to imagine what those blessings will be. I am surrounded by your angels and the Holy Spirit is powerful within me, so how can I be anything else but happy and full of joy. Hallelujah to your wonderful name. Jesus. Jesus. Jesus. Amen.*

# I

# INTUITION

I once published an article, saying that intuition and faith were a great duo. If you have not met your own intuition, you should. It is at work all the time, but you have probably been ignoring it. We are God-equipped, to make it through this trying life. I bet that the people of old relied on it a lot, especially those who did not call Jehovah their God. Intuition must have been very active in the jungles of the world, to help us predict what was around the corner and how to deal with every strange human, animal or plant.

In today's concrete, glass and technological jungle, I dare say, we need intuition just as much. It won't hurt to nurture it. Let's call it 'listening to your inner voice'. It's there to alert you to what is against or for your best interest. It even helps you to say what you did not know you wanted to say. When it works, we are shocked - as if a stranger just leapt in front of us. Wake up that God-given intuition in dealing with people at work, on the street and in relationships and save yourself. Intuition is our invisible eye. That's insight and discernment.

## Bible Verse:

For wisdom will enter your heart, and knowledge will be pleasant to your soul. Discretion will protect you, and understanding will guard you. Wisdom will save you from the ways of wicked men, from men whose words are perverse. **Proverbs 2:10-12**

## Prayer:

*Loving Father, thank you for equipping us with so many good things, like an auto-immune system that works well until we interfere with it, like our self-healing skin, and like the intuition that you impart to us. Help me to listen to that quiet murmur that tells me to leave, to go, to stop, to start or to turn around and let me trust it. I know that since you created me, and you put intuition in me, the Holy Spirit will guide me. All my thoughts and ideas I surrender to your wisdom and power and praise you for all outcomes now and forever more. Amen.*

# INTENTIONS

When we spoke about goals, I had to refrain from speaking about Intentions because intentions are part and parcel of the picture. Intentions take you to a higher level. Usually when the word 'intention' is used, it is understood to mean – what is the outcome you want or what is the real motive behind your action. However, see intention in a more powerful light. See intention as the energy that you hold behind your goals to ensure that you do achieve them.

Intention requires greater focus and consistency. It requires commitment to the goal. That intention must also be fully positive and unwavering, or you will likely sabotage your own goal. Give energy to your intention by charging it with constant, confident, wise and creative thoughts. Your goals and success depend on greater energetic focus to your thoughts and goals.

## Bible Verse:

To humans belong the plans of the heart, but from the Lord comes the proper answer of the tongue. All a person's ways seem pure to them, but motives are weighed by the Lord. Commit to the Lord whatever you do, and he will establish your plans. **Proverbs 16:1-3**

## Prayer:

*Jehovah Nisi, give me the same thoughts as your thoughts. Help me to surrender to your wisdom. I pray that my intentions be strong toward my goals and that they be unselfish in every way. Help me to think and plan in ways that support your will for my life, even though I know that you can do all things, even when I miss the mark. Let my vision and actions be aligned with what is your best plan for me. Thank you for the Holy Spirit which whispers within me constantly, giving me renewed confidence and energy to accomplish what I am here to do. I praise your Holy Name and bow to you, Holy Majesty. Amen.*

# J

## JOY

If we could choose among a hundred positive things to have, I would choose JOY – next to WISDOM, that is. Being joyful for no visible reason and not being able to explain it, is an awesome way to be. As you must have learned: the joy of the Lord is our strength. It may look like you do not care, when you are in joy and others are distressed, but you cannot help it when you have risen to that level where all your cares are cast on Him and you are enjoying divine favor.

It would be good if everyone knew not to aim for things, but for joy. Joy is part of the infrastructure of the Kingdom of God and that is why the Word says: Seek ye first the Kingdom of God, and all these things will be added unto you. JOY is one of them.

## Bible Verse:

I have told you this so that my joy may be in you and that your joy may be complete. **John 15:11**

## Prayer:

*Jehovah Shammah, I thank you that you are the source of my joy. I celebrate your unfailing presence in my life. Forgive me when I doubt that what I desire will manifest in good time and let that interfere with my joy in you. I thank you for the joy of praising you each day that I awake.  I pray that my faith will override my doubts and keep my joy active, no matter what I am faced with. I know that I can trust you, dear God, and so I keep rejoicing in your power and your love. I want your joy to be my strength every single day. This I pray in the name of my Lord and Savior, Jesus Christ. Amen.*

# JEALOUSY

How can you help but be jealous when others have exactly what you want, or what you think you are entitled to, and you do not have? Envy is a relative. Jealousy has controlled thousands in personal and love relationships, in business and work relationships, in financial deals, in conflict between neighbors and in every other human association possible. Even animals are jealous. God says that He is a jealous God, but His jealousy is well-founded.

Your faith may be such that you are able to face losing while others win, failing while others succeed, waiting while others seem to be having it all, and not be bothered by it at all. That would be an enviable state to be in.

If you find yourself bothered by perceived delays in blessings you are expecting, you will have to do a lot of self-talk to walk through and continue praying. Jealousy tarnishes your approach to other people, situations and choices, especially if you are not aware that you are motivated by jealousy. Therefore, you add more pain to your life. Jealousy needs the treatment of 'trust in God', who freely gives everything to us all, as His Word says.

## Bible Verse:

You desire but do not have, so you kill. You covet but you cannot get what you want, so you quarrel and fight. You do not have because you do not ask God. When you ask, you do not receive, because you ask with wrong motives, that you may spend what you get on your pleasures. **James 4:2-3**

## Prayer:

*Loving God, I am ashamed of being jealous. How can I be jealous when I know that you provide, you shower me with your favor every day and you have given me Salvation and all my earthly needs from my birth to today? Jehovah God, El Shaddai, you are all-sufficient, and you promise to bless me abundantly, so help me to see more clearly and trust you to reveal what is your will for me. I am believing that everything that I need or want, which is good for me, you will provide, because you own the whole Universe. Your love for me is greater than imaginable. I rejoice in your Almighty care, as I humbly wait on you. I praise your Holy Name. Amen.*

# K

## KNOWLEDGE

We may equate knowledge with riches. Who knows wins.
However, knowledge is not wisdom, as you will see.
Insider-information is knowledge, knowledge that may be
illegally used, which would be unwise. Knowledge is an
accumulation of facts, figures, data and understanding in
your head, managed by your brain, your human computer.
For the most part, those who don't read or study know
less than those who do. Those who travel and are
observant and curious usually know more about the
world.

Knowledge allows us to make smart moves and see more
options for a better life. Knowledge is the root of
innovations and changes which move societies forward in
different fields, such as science, technology, architecture
etc. You are at an advantage, undoubtedly, with
knowledge, including that of the Word of God. However,
you also need to be wise.

## Bible Verse:

My son, if you accept my words and store up my commandments within you, turning your ear to wisdom and applying your heart to understanding - indeed, if you call out for insight and cry aloud for understanding, and if you look for it as for silver and search for it as for hidden treasures, then you will understand the fear of the LORD and find the knowledge of God.  **Proverbs 2: 1-5**

## Prayer:

*O Good and Gracious God, listen to my cry today as I try to master what I am studying. I know that all knowledge is contained in you. I know that you knew me and all things before the beginning of time and you know everything to come. I want to draw on this great knowledge which transcends anything that scientists or thinkers know. Help me to understand what's difficult to decipher or retain. Guide me to increase my intellect and my value. Let me share my knowledge with others too, and advance your Kingdom. Amen.*

# KINGDOM BUSINESS

I would not attempt to explain God's Kingdom, but I know that our ultimate task is to work for that Kingdom. Whatever we do or achieve should, in all its details, serve the purpose of God's Kingdom. As the verse quoted shows, the Kingdom is us all – both those who have accepted Jesus and those who need to be reached with the Gospel. Our daily tasks are Kingdom Business – the people we touch and the problems we solve. I don't know if everyone is on the same page, when we speak of the 'kingdom business', because Christians often give lip service to that and then go about doing their own business.

However, if we bear in mind that whatever we do should be unto the Lord, not unto ourselves or for show, then we are busy with Kingdom Business. When I offer to pray at a secular meeting or lunch, I am doing Kingdom Business. As a lay person how you operate, all the time, with God in mind, is doing Kingdom Business.

## Bible Verse:

Once, on being asked by the Pharisees when the kingdom of God would come, Jesus replied, "the coming of the kingdom of God is not something that can be observed, nor will people say, 'Here it is,' or 'There it is,' because the kingdom of God is in your midst." **Luke 17:20-21**

## Prayer:

*Jehovah Tsidkenu, God my righteousness, let me reflect your righteousness so that your Kingdom will come, and your Will may be done all around me. Let me be conscious that I am always part of your Kingdom plan and act accordingly. Give me courage to share your grace and power and knowledge with others. Let me spend my days serving your Kingdom and your purpose for us all. Help me teach others to surrender to your Will and find real fulfillment in your service. Let me not miss my chances to serve. I humbly pray all this, in the name of Jesus. Amen.*

# WHAT THE BIBLE CONFIRMS ABOUT THE POWER OF PRAYER

'The prayer of a righteous person is powerful and effective.' **James 5:16**

Thanks for reading and praying thus far. Now, I would like to share with you what the New Testament and the teaching of Jesus and His disciples have to say about prayer, which will serve as ongoing reminders to pray. Of course, you know that the whole Bible is filled with demonstrations of the power of prayer and faith in turning circumstances around. David, above all, seemed to spend his whole life in prayer. His prayers were not all recorded as songs or poetry, which we call the Psalms. I am sure that his prayers were also private, between him and God, as he battled what was in him and around him and became 'a man after God's own heart'.

In the New Testament, all who were healed, I am sure, were praying in their hearts for Jesus to arrive on the scene and rescue them and they acted on their faith and either called out to him or sent for Him. Please take note that the stories we know are the stories we have been told. We have no idea about all the other miracles that were performed in the thousands, as Jesus walked about, and His power went out of Him to those who reached for His mercy.

**The Lord Jesus himself – King of Kings and Lord of Lords - found it necessary to go apart and pray, to build up His spiritual muscles, and was disappointed when He came back from His retreat and found His disciples sleeping.** He was disappointed that they did not understand the urgency and power of praying continuously. *"In these days he went out to the mountain to pray, and all night he continued in prayer to God."* **Luke 6:12**

Here are just a few of those verses. Get curious and find the rest. Note when you read the Bible what happened to women and men, throughout, who stopped to pray through their dilemmas.

## PRAYERS SHOULD BE MESHED WITH GRATEFULNESS AS WE FACE ANXIETIES

Do not be anxious about anything, but in everything by prayer and supplication with thanksgiving let your requests be made known to God. **Philippians 4:6**

## PRAYERS WILL BE ANSWERED IF WE ABIDE IN JESUS

If you abide in me, and my words abide in you, ask whatever you wish, and it will be done for you. **John 15:7**

## PRAYER SHOULD BE UNENDING

Pray without ceasing. **1 Thessalonians 5:17**

## PRAYERS ARE INTERPRETED, REWORDED AND DELIVERED BY THE HOLY SPIRIT

Likewise, the Spirit helps us in our weakness. For we do not know what to pray for as we ought, but the Spirit himself intercedes for us with groanings too deep for words. **Romans 8:26**

## PRAYER IN PRIVATE IS HEARD AND ANSWERED BY GOD

But when you pray, go into your room and shut the door and pray to your Father who is in secret. And your Father who sees in secret will reward you. **Matthew 6:6**

## PRAYER IS ENCOURAGED BY JESUS FOR THOSE WHO ARE DEPRESSED

And he told them a parable to the effect that they ought always to pray and not lose heart. **Luke 18:1**

## PRAYER SHOULD BE ACCOMPANIED BY FAITH TO GET RESULTS

And whatever you ask in prayer, you will receive, if you have faith." **Matthew 21:22**

## PRAYER SHOULD INVOLVE OUR MIND AND OUR SPIRIT

What am I to do? I will pray with my spirit, but I will pray with my mind also; I will sing praise with my spirit, but I will sing with my mind also. **1 Corinthians 14:15**

## PRAYER SHOULD NOT BE EMPTY AND FOR SHOW

"And when you pray, do not heap up empty phrases as the Gentiles do, for they think that they will be heard for their many words. **Matthew 6:7**

## PRAYER SHOULD BE MADE CONFIDENTLY WHEN WE ARE IN NEED

Let us then with confidence draw near to the throne of grace, that we may receive mercy and find grace to help in time of need. **Hebrews 4:16**

## PRAYER IS THE ONLY WAY OUT OF CERTAIN DEADLY DILEMMAS

And he said to them, "This kind cannot be driven out by anything but prayer." **Mark 9:29**

## PRAYER IS RECOMMENDED FOR EVERYONE, THE GREAT, AND THE LOWLY

First of all, then, I urge that supplications, prayers, intercessions, and thanksgivings be made for all people, for kings and all who are in high positions, that we may lead a peaceful and quiet life, godly and dignified in every way.

But I call to God, and the LORD will save me. Evening and morning and at noon I utter my complaint and moan, and he hears my voice. **1 Timothy 2:1-2**

## PRAYERS OF THE GODLY ARE LIKE PERFUME TO GOD

And another angel came and stood at the altar with a golden censer, and he was given much incense to offer with the prayers of all the saints on the golden altar before the throne, and the smoke of the incense, with the prayers of the saints, rose before God from the hand of the angel. **Revelation 8:3-4**

## THE PRAYER TRAJECTORY THAT WORKS
"**Ask** and it will be given to you; **seek** and you will find; **knock** and the door will be opened to you." For everyone who asks receives; the one who seeks finds; and to the one who knocks, the door will be opened. **Matthew 7:7-12**

## PERSISTENCE IN PRAYER

The Parable of the Persistent Widow

**Then Jesus told his disciples a parable to show them that they should always pray and not give up**. He said: 'In a certain town there was a judge who neither feared God nor cared what people thought. And there was a widow in that town who kept coming to him with the plea, 'Grant me justice against my adversary.'

"For some time he refused. But finally he said to himself, 'Even though I don't fear God or care what people think, yet because this widow keeps bothering me, I will see that she gets justice, so that she won't eventually come and attack me!'"

And the Lord said, "Listen to what the unjust judge says. **And will not God bring about justice for his chosen ones, who cry out to him day and night?** Will he keep putting them off? I tell you, he will see that they get justice, and quickly. However, when the Son of Man comes, will he find faith on the earth?" **Luke 18: 1-8**

# L

## LOVE

Love is like a drug. Love and hate seem to be related, even though they appear as opposite emotions. God is love. How do we reconcile all of this? I believe when we truly love someone, it is the God in them that we see. To us they represent God – as far as we can see. We get angrier with those we love because we expect, in the exchange of love, that only what is good, pure and lovely will appear. How misdirected we are, especially in romantic love.

Still, love is curative. Love of a spouse, a child or other person puts us through a variety of tests, so do not be shocked when hell happens despite the love. Love must be learned, and love needs to be nurtured. We disappoint our loving God when we ignore Him, blame Him, reject Him and even deny Him, but He loves us still, so that we come out 'more than conquerors'. We speak of 'being in love' but it is better yet to be a 'love being', who projects and attracts love.

## Bible Verse:

"The most important one," answered Jesus, "is this: 'Hear, O Israel: The Lord our God, the Lord is one. Love the Lord your God with all your heart and with all your soul and with all your mind and with all your strength.' The second is this: 'Love your neighbor as yourself.' There is no other commandment greater than these."
**Mark 12:29-31**

## Prayer:

*Lord, teach me what love is. I am ignorant. Teach me to love myself, first. Teach me to love you although I can never match your love. Forgive me for withholding my love from others. Thank you for the love of my parents and for the love I have been able to share with my spouse as well as my children. Let love multiply in my life. Let the love in my heart be the weapon by which I conquer in all battles. Help me to show others how to love, by my giving, my forgiving and my compassion. Forgive us all for being ungenerous with that same love that you have so generously given us. By the blood of Jesus, I pray. Amen.*

# LAZINESS

It is amazing how many people are just lazing around doing nothing and then say - What is happening? The world is going to pieces. Are you contributing or facilitating the problem? Laziness is not limited to one class or group of people. There are tons of white collar, educated and connected persons who are earning high income for a lifetime, without producing anything significant in the society. They are lazy in intellect and in spirit, because they are thinking and acting selfishly. Laziness is exhibited when we do less than what is required or drag out a task which could be done in a timelier manner.

It's ok to feel lazy sometimes about something which does not interest you, but laziness should not be your normal modus operandi in life. Mothers have official permit to be lazy after tiring hours of multitasking for years. Lazy, distracted students risk not graduating, not ultimately getting employed, and not keeping a job if they do get one. Help them to change. Lazy men who watch women folk wear themselves ragged, doing triple duty, are an abomination. Let's get busy.

## Bible Verse:

Lazy hands make for poverty, but diligent hands bring wealth. **Proverbs 10:4**

## Prayer:

*Father in Heaven, help us all to be diligent. Let us apply our energy to what is truly important and not to what looks good or will bring us acclaim for a while. Let us not be lazy in bringing your message to those to whom you send us. Let us be speedy in doing your will. Save us from sluggishness when there should be urgency on our part, in our families, in our communities, in the workplace and in the church. In the great and redeeming name of Jesus, we pray. Amen.*

## MONEY

There is so much talk about money, and I shiver to talk about it here. Money was sticks and stones and then made its way to become paper and then plastic. Money doesn't even exist, yet we work hard for it. When you make an electronic transfer, what passes through the wires? Anything? I know it's all backed up by gold, but ultimately, what is exchanged? Anything? Money is an idea. The Bible is right: Come buy without money.  Income is generated from ideas. Others are convinced that what we are selling – designs, products, experiences, services, etc.- is worth their while or resources, so they pay. Hopes are shot or raised, based on loss or prospect of money.

The earliest Church shared their wealth in common so that they could all have enough to eat and thrive. That practice has not prevailed. Money will always dwindle, when it is not spent the way it should be. Today, saving is at 0.00% interest. Is the money resting or rusting then? God promises to bless us going in and coming out while the world's systems rob us, going in and coming out. If we seek after righteousness first, we are promised that all things will be added onto us – including financial wealth.

## Bible Verse:

Command those who are rich in this present world not to be arrogant nor to put their hope in wealth, which is so uncertain, but to put their hope in God, who richly provides us with everything for our enjoyment. Command them to do good, ... In this way they will lay up treasure for themselves as a firm foundation....., so that they may take hold of the life that is truly life. **1 Timothy 6:17-19**

## Prayer:

*Jehovah God, even though I do not have much, I know that I can be as guilty as someone rich who worships money and is not ready to share. Give me the faith to put you to the test, as you ask, and give my tithes and offerings to bless your work. I ask you to do what you promise and 'open the windows of heaven' and pour out many blessings on me. I want to rejoice in the financial as well as spiritual overflow in my life. I rejoice and praise you now for what I know is already on the way for my family and all loved ones. In the name of my Lord and Savior, I pray. Amen.*

# MARRIAGE

Marriage is not the wedding. My marriage lasted 40 years – until death did us part. It did not depend on how wonderful the wedding was. Marriage always depends on who the partners are and how conscious they are of God's role in it. Over the centuries marriages have been made based on very faulty premises and expectations and yet everyone expects the perfect result, or do they? If there is little love being shared in a marriage, disaster is lurking in the bushes. Is that too hard to see? Impatience does not work in any marriage. Selfishness and marriage do not work together.

Marriage is an arrangement which God saw fit to establish, to allow us all to multiply, not just in child-bearing and child-rearing, but to multiply in the sense of expanding our abilities, mindset, contribution to the planet and to His Kingdom.

Within most marriages today, there is far less safety, joy, provision, progress than intended to be, in such an unmatchable arrangement devised by God. Turn to God for His help, not to another man or woman.

## Bible Verse:

Husbands, love your wives, just as Christ loved the church and gave himself up for her, to make her holy, …., and to present her to himself as a radiant church, …holy and blameless…In this same way, husbands ought to love their wives as their own bodies. He who loves his wife loves himself. **Ephesians 5:25-28**

## Prayer:

*Sweet smelling praise we raise to you now, Lord, thanking you for guiding us in choosing each other. We are trusting you that you have a greater plan for our lives than we can imagine, as we face these number of difficulties. Lord, help us when we hurt or feel inadequate in this relationship. Forgive us when we are intolerant. Cleanse us of our unrighteous and fearful thoughts. Lord, we give you the full right and access to turn things around and keep us rejoicing in your favor. Help us love each other with the same love that you are offering to us. Forgive us where we are failing and keep us humble and loving toward each other, our beloved. We graciously ask, celebrating life with you, our Savior and Lord. Amen.*

# N

## NATURE

I've seen nature from many sides of the world. You are looking at nature when you visit a zoo. You see nature arranged in botanical gardens worldwide, in home gardens and out in the wild, and each time there is a surprise, if you are looking. Museums are full of fossils of animal varieties both extinct and living today. The intricacies of nature, with comical looking plants and flowers resembling animals in a variety of colors and hues, all reflect the masterful art of the Creator.

Nature is reflected in different colors of the earth, for example, in Mauritius. The waterfalls and caverns of the world, the underwater population and the creatures flying overhead are all God's artistry, beauty and love. He made it all for us to enjoy and we go ahead and destroy them or take them for granted. There is a war for and against belief in Climate Change. Who will cry last? While they talk and quibble to preserve industry and money, islands are getting more vulnerable to be washed away and erosions are taking place depleting regions of food and livelihood. Preserve nature where you are.  Remember we need the oxygen and the honey.

## Bible Verse:

"But ask the animals, and they will teach you, or the birds in the sky, and they will tell you; or speak to the earth, and it will teach you, or let the fish in the sea inform you. Which of all these does not know that the hand of the LORD has done this? In his hand is the life of every creature and the breath of all mankind. **Job 12:7-10**

## Prayer:

*Teach us to honor Nature, dear Jehovah Jireh. You have provided us with everything we need to be in health and to prosper and we think we are so smart that we deplete and destroy what is for our own good. Help us not only to take care of nature but to stop and admire and enjoy it and teach all children to do the same. Thank you, Sweet Jesus, for this great advantage of a vibrant life of fresh air, the beauty of nature and energy to live. Amen.*

# NEXT STEP

If you are alive at all and eager to be competent about anything in which you are involved at home or at work, the question should always arise as to 'what's next'. When we have goals and intentions, executing them requires continuous next steps. In our spiritual walk too, there are next steps to take because we are reaching toward perfection. If there are no next steps, then there will be no growth. When we are learning, questions will always be: what do I do next? When we are at a level of mastery in any area of life or study, it is up to us to determine our 'next step' to advance, to expand and to become more expert at what we do.

If our goal is excellence, then we will be weighing and balancing what we do and not be purely reacting to criticism or to missteps. Never think that you have 'arrived', especially in doing God's work. Learning and innovating is without limit.

# Bible Verse:

All Scripture is God-breathed....so that the servant of God may be thoroughly equipped for every good work.
**II Timothy 3:16-17**

# Prayer:

*Sweet, wonderful Lord and Master, I bow before you to ask for you to listen to my prayer. I thank you for every breath of air we breathe. I thank you for fresh, clean water. I thank you for the roof over our heads and income to pay my bills. Now I seek to know what my next step should be. Lord, I ask you to direct my steps as you directed the men and women who worshipped you in the Bible including Ruth and Naomi, Hannah, Esther, David, Daniel and the Disciples.*

*I know that my next steps need to be ordered by you, so I wait for your guidance. Let be not be haughty in moving forward or changing course. Let me be more eager to hear from you than to just do something new. I wait with expectation for your wonderful surprises. In Jesus's name. Amen.*

# OPPORTUNITY

In this age of multi-media and high and intricate technologies, there are so many opportunities – to learn, to create, to earn, to reach others around the globe, and to do evil like hacking, catfishing and scamming the vulnerable. These verses from Ephesians 5 could be written directly for this age: *Look carefully then how you walk, not as unwise but as wise, making the best use of the time, because the days are evil. Therefore, do not be foolish, but understand what the will of the Lord is. And do not get drunk with wine, for that is debauchery, but be filled with the Spirit, addressing one another in psalms and hymns and spiritual songs, singing and making melody to the Lord with your heart, ...'* What opportunities are you seizing today?

With all the options out there, there are not enough income-earning opportunities for the majority of people. Opportunities have been deliberately stolen from generations of people because of racial discrimination. However, we should learn to create our own opportunities by seeing new ways to use old things, and new services to render to the changing demographics in every community. Each new trend is started because someone thought to offer a product that shifts people's vision, of how things should be done. Finally, be the one to create an opportunity for others.

## Bible Verse:

Be wise in the way you act toward outsiders; make the most of every opportunity. **Colossians 4:5**

## Prayer:

*Dear loving God, please open the doors of opportunity for me, as I seek to advance and succeed in my efforts. You know what I do and how dedicated I am to my tasks, the time I spend developing my skills and gifts. I need the right opportunities to turn up for my efforts. Please, forgive me for failing to recognize your generous hand and for missing the opportunities you send. Open my eyes to the possibilities and give me the drive and perseverance to pursue great opportunities. I praise you for all the good gifts you provide. I receive now in Jesus's name. Amen.*

# ORDER

Is the United States in order, is the world in order? Certainly not. Are our households in order, hmm-mm? God gave us a world in full order. Creation happened step by step, day by day and it has not had to be redone. Order is essential on the outside in order not to influence the inside, and order is essential on the inside because it will be reflected on the outside. It's a tango. How we constantly think creates our outer world and how the world responds to us, and the way we allow ourselves to live generates the feelings and the energy by which we operate. Everyone knows that getting rid of clutter makes you feel better.

CLEARING CLUTTER spiritually and physically opens room for more, gets rid of what's not needed, and clears the mind. It's important for children to learn to declutter their zones and experience this too. Ghettos are where people keep looking at STAGNATION and see no way out. Even those with money get bogged down in disorder as they arrogantly turn from legitimate business to criminal, controlling activities and abusive behavior, demeaning others. Keep order.

# Bible Verse:

But everything should be done in a fitting and orderly way.  **1 Corinthians 14:40**

# Prayer:

*Great God of Righteousness, who is Holy, Holy, Holy. We praise you for not leaving us to our own devices, for not seeing us covered in our sins but covered by the blood of Jesus.  Father, thank you for your Word, which leads us like a lamp in the dark. Let me not allow chaos to take over, dear Father. Let me inspire order wherever I go. Let me live at that higher level of consciousness where I think straight and my whole life reflects divine order and blesses everyone around me. I pray this in the precious name of your Son, Jesus Christ. Amen.*

## POWER

Power struggles take place outright, or subtly, in every walk of life – in the village, in the city, in Government and in any organization or group where there is organized leadership and management involved. That outer power game is so energy- and time-consuming and usually results in more loss than gain, for all. Enemies are created and those who should benefit are left disappointed. That happens even in the Church. Abominable.

The power we really need is that of managing our own selves, our minds and our spirits. The power that God wants us to be exercising is doing the work which Jesus started, so that we do 'greater works' than He did. The word 'empowerment' has been thrown around everywhere for a good while, but people act that out as a battle against others, rather than as personal and inner enhancement. Power is not for corporate executives and mega-transnational corporations.

Power is for the saints of God to influence what transpires on this planet minute by minute. Let's grab hold of power through faith, prayer and calling into being on earth, what is already in existence in heaven.

## Bible Verse:

You, God, are awesome is your sanctuary; the God of Israel gives power and strength to his people. Praise be to God! **Psalm 68:35**

## Prayer:

*Mighty God, consume us with your power. Let me feel your power surrounding me. I know your power is too great for us to endure. You are so awesome. How could we handle even an ounce of your power within us? However, Lord, let us taste of it as we pray privately, as we pray in our families and churches. Dear God, what is missing is your all-consuming power. I ask for your empowerment for every task I undertake and for every action I take today and always. I pray in the overcoming name of Jesus, my Savior. Amen.*

# PEACE

I love peace. I have felt peace in several situations when
normally I should have felt turmoil and upset, and I even
questioned why.  Was that peace or detachment? Peace is
a state that should be cultivated. The emergency rooms
are filled with us all who have lost or never known peace
or had our peace interrupted.  Nations deliberate every
day in bilateral and multilateral forums, and iron out
deals, to ensure that peace prevails between them, and
within them, but the struggle for peace continues because
each day new conflicts erupt. The world reflects the
personal lack of peace of all its people. Each day that level
of rage escalates and swallows up more victims. What can
we contribute to peace, other than fundraising events?
Peaceful sports events erupt into violent fighting and
raging lunacy. Are our thoughts peaceful enough to keep
us healthy, create our calm surroundings and influence
the world? Keep praying for peace, as we see generations
running as desperate refugees all over the world, due to
evil despots.

## Bible Verse:

Do not be anxious about anything, but in every situation, by prayer and petition, with thanksgiving, present your requests to God. And the peace of God, which transcends all understanding, will guard your hearts and your minds in Christ Jesus. **Philippians 4:6-7**

## Prayer:

*Divine Lord, give me your peace. Keep me in peace. Let me not be distressed by passing circumstances when I know that you have the best plans ahead for me. Give me the gift of helping others to find peace when they are bothered by what they are experiencing. Let my faith be strong enough to keep me focused on you and not on current situations. Show me how to make peace envelope my life and create a heavenly atmosphere for me and all around me. I place my trust in you now and always. In Jesus's precious name, I pray. Amen.*

## QUESTIONS

I have published a whole article, on the matter of questions, in which I itemized questions, which we should ask ourselves strategically, to manage a multitude of challenges in our lives. My main point was that many of the answers we seek are in the very questions which we may ask ourselves, if we are ready to listen.  Ask yourself questions which, if someone else asked you, you would be hard-pressed to answer truthfully. Speak the truth to yourself. On the other hand, don't be afraid to seek answers from other sources. The Bible recommends seeking counsel.

Questions are not only good for our own personal needs, but for societal ones as well, so that you are less likely to be duped, or to become anxious over false news. God will answer, whether we ask for things or about things, so pose your most urgent questions anytime, just like the Psalmist David often did.

## Bible Verse:

I say to God, my rock: "Why have you forgotten me? Why must I go mourning, oppressed by the enemy?" **Psalm 42:9**

## Prayer:

*Heavenly Father, I come to you with questions and I wait for your answers. I know that you answer immediately because you hear me, but I may have to wait to see the answers or understand them. I humbly ask you, Lord, should I just endure, or should I be fighting my way out of this situation? Am I supposed to always be that 'good soldier of Jesus Christ' and not get a break to enjoy my life? If I love you Lord and you love me, why do I have to go through all this pain and headache? I want to praise you, but I don't feel like it because I feel cheated and I know that there is better for me. Show me how I can cooperate with your will and receive the blessings that you have for me. I pray in faith in Jesus's name. Amen.*

# QUALITY

There's nothing worse than spending money to buy something that you really like and then it turns out to be poorly made or not worth what you spent. All manufacturers give at least lip-service to the quality and care with which their products are made, but the proof is in the using.  Even food products cannot be trusted these days, as to whether they are healthy enough, void of carcinogens or prepared under sanitary conditions.

Quality applies not only to things but to actual service and communication with each other. Every classroom should emphasize quality and teachers should fully demonstrate that. People in charge need to be as concerned about the quality of behavior toward their subordinates as much as subordinates should be toward their supervisors. Fast-food service should display as much quality as 5-star, 5-course dinner service. Food is being served for entry into a human body. Even more so, the quality of interaction and of output from Christians and the Church should be significantly higher than those of others or elsewhere. Let's consider that.

## Bible Verse:

Their work will be shown for what it is, because the Day will bring it to light. It will be revealed with fire, and the fire will test the quality of each person's work.
**1 Corinthians 3:13**

## Prayer:

*Dear Father in Heaven, help us to aim for the best as we prepare to give service on our jobs, in our business and in our homes. Let us give of our best even when no one is watching over our shoulders or holding us accountable. Let us serve you above everything else with all our hearts and minds so that we truly help to make your Kingdom come. Let us study your word diligently and let us pray fervently as your Word tells us to do. Let our lives be synonymous with quality, no matter how little or how much we have. Help us, Lord, to set the example for quality everywhere, and teach this way of life to our children as they grow. Amen.*

# R

## REPENTANCE

Repentance sounds like a scary proposition to the sinner. When you have not reconciled with Christ and accepted him as Lord of your life, when someone proposes that you need to repent, it sounds like an affront. At least, that is the way I suspect it was, when I heard the word being used by preachers and teachers of the Gospel. I don't hear the word 'repentance' being used too much these days but the proposition is still the same: you must repent and be baptized. You must confess your sins and declare that you are turning around and going the way dictated by Jesus Christ. The proposition is not that you just – try to be good and hope for the best. Repentance is the starting point, even if you feel like you really have nothing to be forgiven for. We are all born unforgiven, let's just put it out like that.

To move forward to where we can please God and have his full divine favor we must be redeemed. That is step one to ensuring a place in the eternal Kingdom of Light. If nothing else moves you, let the message of repentance do. The blood of Jesus and His sacrifice provided the opportunity for you to repent once and for all.

## Bible Verse:

The Lord is not slow in keeping his promise, as some understand slowness. Instead he is patient with you, not wanting anyone to perish, but everyone to come to repentance. **II Peter 3:9**

## Prayer:

*Great, wonderful God, today I bow before you. Thank you for pointing the light on my path and opening this new understanding to me that I need to repent. Thank you for sending your son, Jesus Christ, the Righteous One, to die on the cross of Calvary for my sins and the sins of the whole world. Today, I accept Jesus as my Lord and only Savior and I look to Him to reveal himself in my life daily. I praise you for the Holy Spirit with which you will fill me today, to keep and protect me as I bless your Holy Name. Amen. Hallelujah.*

# RESTORATION

As a Life and Career Coach I collaborate with coachees about re-inventing themselves, to advance, find better job satisfaction or earn better income. God offers us the daily opportunity of restoring our souls since we sin every day and drift off the path. The restoration of art work is a very skilled and painstaking job. The restoration of homes and buildings which are considered valuable takes a lot of effort and money. To a far greater extent the restoration of our spirit and soul takes a great deal of effort and striving, especially when we have really fallen in the dumps. We often do not forgive ourselves or forgive others, so that makes the restoration process last longer. It is not that God is not ready or willing.

Relationships in families, in groups, in communities and countries are broken in a variety of ways that last for years or centuries, without the restoration which is badly needed. Many have experienced relationships broken without any chance of restoration, called divorce. Being restored gives everyone another fighting chance to begin again and move ahead without old burdens. God's saving Grace does exactly that, both when we first receive his Salvation and throughout our Christian lives.

## Bible Verse:

Finally, brothers and sisters, rejoice! Strive for
full restoration, encourage one another, be of one mind,
live in peace. And the God of love and peace will be with
you. **II Corinthians 13:11**

## Prayer:

*Divine Lord, Yahweh, listen to my cry today.  I am
humbling myself under your almighty wings of love which
you offer to all, without preference for one or the other. I
beg you to restore what I have lost. I don't even want the
same, I want greater. I want only what you want for me
because your plans and purpose for me are far better and
I only want to depend on you. Especially, Lord, restore my
spirit so that I can truly smile and live joyfully no matter
where I am and with whom I am. I praise you for your
Grace in this regard and receive your makeover now.
Amen.*

# S

## SADNESS

We live in a sad world.  People reach for help from pills and the bottle, as we know. That seems to be an easier source of relief than looking up to the God and Redeemer of our life, or going through an internal healing process. Sadness being the opposite of joy, weakens us. Sadness can be brought on by our thoughts rather than by an actual, current event, as well as by empathizing with the suffering of others. Grief, on the passing of a loved one, may keep you crying for months, as I have experienced, and reliving the pain over a protracted period.

In addition, your soul may be sad even without grief, loss or pain from abuse. You may be saddened in feeling deeply alone, abandoned, threatened or unloved – whether real or imagined. No one can function at any acceptable level if buried inside in sadness, but that is the emotional state in families, in communities and across the globe – among both children and adults and even among the clergy and their families.

The Church may be busy and appear to be flourishing, without really winning the souls that God wants to adopt as His children. That should make us sad in these days.

# Bible Verse:

I waited patiently for the LORD; he turned to me and heard my cry. He lifted me out of the slimy pit, out of the mud and mire; he set my feet on a rock and gave me a firm place to stand. He put a new song in my mouth, a hymn of praise to our God. Many will see and fear the Lord and put their trust in him.  **Psalm 40:1-3**

# Prayer:

*Great, loving Father in Heaven, we are recipients of your great mercy every day. Make us worthy. In my sadness today, I ask for the Holy Spirit's intervention to create a new heart and mind within me, so that I can be free of this feeling. I can't help but be sad, but I want to believe even more in your grace and tender care for me. I want to be rejoicing in your love, more than succumbing to my pain. I feel robbed. I feel punished, but I know that you know best. I wait to be transformed. Cover me now, Lord Jesus. I receive, as I weep and wait. Amen.*

# SUCCESS

What's my measure of success may not be yours. Nevertheless, I think most humans know the signs of prosperity when we see them – bigger, larger, grander, longer, more expensive, plenteous of whatever. Success depends on what you are aiming for or what you value. What someone who is dedicated to fishing is aiming at, waiting for hours with his baits, is different from the executive maneuvering to close a contract or to snatch business from a competitor. Just getting out of poverty, without any trappings of riches, is high success for many.

Many people enjoy the experience of success from intellectual accomplishment and still others are so satisfied by spiritual pursuit that 'success' is not even considered. Very skilled and talented people lead a modest lifestyle because they find fulfillment and success in the very quality of the activity in which they are engaged, and not in financial reward. Don't be driven by what others call success. Just make sure that you have GOOD SUCCESS, the kind the Bible espouses.

## Bible Verse:

The LORD was with Joseph so that he prospered, and he lived in the house of his Egyptian master.  When his master saw that the LORD was with him and that the LORD gave him success in everything he did, Joseph found favor in his eyes and became his attendant. Potiphar put him in charge of his household, and he entrusted to his care everything he owned.
**Genesis 39:2-4**

## Prayer:

*Lord and Master, I do know that you want me to prosper, even as my soul prospers and therefore, I come to you in prayer about what I am facing now. You know how hard I work, how I give my all, but I am not making it the way I want to. Lord, am I being too impatient, too faithless? Am I on the wrong path? Dearest Lord, speak to me. I want to hear your voice. Give me the energy to continue and the wisdom to do what will indeed make me succeed. I cast my cares on you, knowing that you care. In Jesus's name. Amen.*

# T

## TOMORROW

Tomorrow will take care of itself, we have read in Matthew 6, but we don't believe it. Some are so scared of tomorrow that they take their own lives. Of course, we know that that happens, triggered by psychological imbalances and drug addictions, among other things. Tomorrow is scary for a mother who must feed her children and has no money in her purse or in the bank, and no one reliable to supply her with money on demand. Tomorrow is scary the day before a job interview, after many previous rejections. Each of us is facing a tomorrow that is either full of expectations and excitement or one full of challenges and unknowns.

We have a God that is begging us to give Him our tomorrows. Do that by faith and maintain your prayer life. Don't run to God only when tomorrow scares you. He is never busy, so please, keep in touch with the one who you want to help you in time of need. Sheer courtesy to your Master.  Always anticipate great things for tomorrow. It holds surprises.

## Bible Verse:

Joshua told the people, "Consecrate yourselves, for **tomorrow** the LORD will do amazing things among you." **Joshua 3:5**

## Prayer:

*Jehovah Shalom, I bring you my tomorrows, all of them, from now until I join you in glory. I need and want your intervention in everything in my life. I know nothing, and all good things come from you. You are the God of Peace, so I want to stay away from turmoil. Today, I need resolution to several things. I am overwhelmed. I do not have enough time, not enough help, not enough money, nor do I know who to trust. That's a lot of unknowns. I ask for guidance and favor. I especially ask that you go before me and make my path straight. I pray in faith, giving thanks to you, dear Father. Amen.*

# TEMPTATION

Have you been tempted to kill someone? That must be the ultimate temptation. Extreme anger! Have you been tempted to give up on God? James tells us: "Let no one say when he is tempted I am being tempted by God, for God cannot be tempted with evil, and he himself tempts no one. But each person is tempted when he is lured and enticed by his own desire." Despite these strong words, we still have the assurance from God in 1 Corinthians of how God has made provision for us to overcome temptation.

Temptation is more commonly associated with greed and stealing or with infidelity between spouses, but temptation lies lurking around all corners in less extreme situations. When we cut corners, or give less than our best, we are reacting to temptation. The devil tempts us when we doubt God's intentions towards us.

Temptation and guilt go together, either during or after the temptation has resulted in action. The quickest relief from temptation is to remember whose we are and who we want to please.

## Bible Verse:

No temptation has overtaken you except what is common to mankind. And God is faithful; he will not let you be tempted beyond what you can bear. But when you are tempted, he will also provide a way out so that you can endure it. **1 Corinthians 10:13**

## Prayer:

*I come into your holy presence right now, Lord, and my mind is fully centered in the power of the Holy Spirit in my life. I ask for cleansing and renewal now as I pray for power over any temptation I may face today. I do not want to displease you and I know that the devil is waiting to distract me and lure me away from you. Let me not be tempted to think the wrong thoughts, make the wrong choices or do the wrong things. Help me not to entertain anger against others. I surrender to your highest thoughts rather than to my flesh, as I trust in Jesus's name. Amen.*

# UNIQUENESS

Our individual skills, talents and qualities are gifts from God. Babies are born equipped and we sometimes observe their gifts very early in their lives, while others develop them slowly. Most of us end up drifting away from that central calling which was intended for us. When we learn to use our gifts and competencies it brings us 'before kings' as the Word says. It also allows us to generate the income that we need and desire.

Our skills are literally handed to us to carry out all the tasks that the world community, as well as the church, needs for wholesome living. Our talents are not by accident. They are God-given gifts. They are connected to our dreams. Let's manifest our uniqueness to its fullest.

## Bible Verse:

For by the grace given to me I say to every one of you: Do not think of yourself more highly than you ought, but rather think of yourself with sober judgment, in accordance with the faith God has distributed to each of you.  For just as each one of us has one body with many members, and these members do not have the same function, so in Christ we, ...We have different gifts, according to the grace given to each of us...
**Romans 12:3-6**

## Prayer:

*Jehovah M'Kaddesh, I know that all my talents and skills come from you. Thank you for all the abilities that you have given us as gifts to use for our own good and the good of others. Help each of my children to enlarge their lives through their gifts. Guide me in what I do and how I use my gifts going forward. Help me build on them and not waste them. Let me not be distracted, but focused. Let me work diligently to maximize my gifts for your glory and to bless others. In the precious name of Jesus, I pray. Amen.*

# UNCERTAINTY

I am sure that you would never agree that a state of uncertainty is a pleasant thing. You would want to exchange uncertainty for assurance and solid direction, but I have news for you. Uncertainty is the path of best prospect. It's when we don't know and are unsure, that we go seeking, that we examine, reflect and evaluate. A test is not a good test if it does not make you feel for a minute that there is something you might not know, if it does not make you think and re-think.

Uncertainty allows us to move away from a lackadaisical approach to living and leads us into creating situations for ourselves, that will leave less and less room for mistakes. Uncertainty allows us to learn and become more assured that we can deal with unknowns, and that we can trust inner wisdom, spiritual guidance and the God who created us.

## Bible Verse:

Therefore I tell you, do not worry about your life, what you will eat or drink; or about your body, what you will wear. Is not life more than food, and the body more than clothes? Look at the birds of the air; they do not sow or reap or store away in barns, and yet your heavenly Father feeds them. Are you not much more valuable than they? Can any one of you by worrying add a single hour to your life? **Matthew 6:25-27**

## Prayer:

*Lord, you know that I do not know what to do, but you are omniscient. You know everything, and you are everywhere. I am thinking through what I must do to get out of this rut which I am in and I can't see any way right now, but I know that there are many ways through. I am trusting you to strengthen me so that I can wait for your revelation. Bring me the solutions that are best for me and let me not do anything to spoil your plans for me. Nothing seems to be going my way, but I am sure that you, dear Loving Father, are ahead of me remolding and transforming. I praise you and thank you for the solutions which I cannot see right now, because you are God alone and you are always good.  Amen.*

# V

## VEXATION

In the American KJV translation of the Bible, we read of 'vexation' of spirit. In the Caribbean, the word 'vex' is used adjectivally to describe the mood you are in, rather than as a verb 'to vex someone'. If you are vexed, you are angry. To have a vexation of your spirit is to be in a horrible place. There is no space for the Spirit of God to work when another spirit has taken over. That means we should get rid of it fast. We may be 'angry and sin not'.

We may be indignant against a wrong, against blatant abuse and so on but not be so riled up that love goes out the window, compassion is forgotten, and peace is foreign to our thoughts. When you are annoyed, try to ask yourself if your whole spirit is vexed, or if your anger is rightly directed to the source of annoyance.

## Bible Verse:

…. As everyone comes, so they depart, and what do they gain, since they toil for the wind? All their days they eat in darkness, with great frustration, affliction and anger. **Ecclesiastes 5:16-17**

## Prayer:

*Father in Heaven, I come before you now in humble prayer. Who am I to be angry and unforgiving to anyone? You have forgiven me for so much and you are still blessing me. Please take away any anger that I may feel toward members of my family and those with whom I work. Lord, I ask you to let me practice compassion and kindness so that I make full room for you and the Holy Spirit to dwell and flourish within me. I lay my angry feelings aside. Please help me not to pick them up again, no matter what the trigger. I bless your Holy Name and praise you, by the mighty name of Jesus. Amen.*

# VANITY

Vanity is akin to pride. Looking in the mirror and thinking more of yourself, as being better, more beautiful and more lovable than others, is the usual image associated with vanity. We spend an inordinate amount of time doing that, even when none of the above applies to us or very little of them. You may be vain but really have no reason to be. We create illusions which help us to live with ourselves.

Neither those who have features and possessions that others could envy nor those who have less to offer superficially, should have need of being vain. Everything belongs to God, so what are you being vain about? We really did not originate anything. We came here empty and we are leaving empty.  The only lasting thing will be our relationship with our God and Redeemer. Hello!

## Bible Verse:

But the LORD said to Samuel, "**Do not consider** his appearance or his height, for I have rejected him. The LORD does not look at the things people look at. People look at the outward appearance, but the LORD looks at the heart." **1 Samuel 16:7**

## Prayer:

*Heavenly Lord of our lives, God of our salvation, keeper of our souls, we thank you for your mercy as we seek to humble ourselves in your presence. You have blessed us so much and we ought to be just praising you and sharing your love and grace with everyone else. Let us practice not looking down at others but seek to build them up and support their desire to be whole and complete before you. Let us get rid of vain thoughts which tarnish our motives and actions. Let us deny ourselves and our fleshy desires, and follow you. For Christ's sake, Amen.*

## WAITING

It is difficult to wait and, yet we must. Life is too short to wait to do things, we often think, and so we rush and make mistakes. One of the most familiar Bible quotes is: Wait and see the salvation of the Lord. God invites us to: *Be still and know that I am God*. No, we know better, so we move on up ahead of Him and make a perfect mess. I often delay action, to see if that action is truly necessary, when I get an urgent request. The urgency is often only in the requestor's head, and not necessary. We should also wait – to allow the process to work when something is being studied, or developed.

The best things are produced, just like the health of our bodies, by allowing day light to shine on them and night time to provide rest. Even when there is an audience waiting for someone to speak or act or sing, a pause before the performer begins is not out of order. Let them wait while the performer gets into form, mentally. Wait, I say, on that ideal job, that life partner, that enviable vacation, and so on!

## Bible Verse:

but those who hope in the LORD will renew their strength. They will soar on wings like eagles; they will run and not grow weary, they will walk and not be faint. **Isaiah 40:31**

## Prayer:

*Jehovah Rohe, my great Shepherd. You are my Lord, and through you I learn to see the wonderful experiences and outcomes that you have provided in advance. As I wait, let me be expectant and believing. Help me surrender to your bigger purpose for my life and the lives of all to whom I am connected. Waiting is difficult, but I will continue to work and pray and trust you each day. When I begin to doubt, nudge me through your Holy Spirit to remember your promises. In Jesus's holy name, I pray. Amen.*

# WISDOM

I adopted the name 'sapience' since I was a teenager in Latin class, to use for any future business, and I have done so. Sapience means wisdom. Wisdom is my favorite thing, alongside vision and I fell in love with Solomon and his wisdom since childhood too.

Wisdom goes beyond knowledge, because it comes from an invisible, all-powerful source in the subtlest of ways, and at the most appropriate moment. It's like the brain and knowing shut down while true wisdom takes over so that your decision, choices and action supersede what is natural or expected.

Wisdom often bypasses rules and common-sense judgment. When we pray we should ask for God's wisdom and not for mere human solutions. That is why some people's ideas are considered – ahead of their time. Being wise is to transcend space and time, in fact. When you act in wisdom, expect others to be baffled or even antagonized.

## Bible Verse:

To the person who pleases him, God gives wisdom, knowledge and happiness, but to the sinner he gives the task of gathering and storing up wealth to hand it over to the one who pleases God. **Ecclesiastes 2:26**

## Prayer:

*Dear God, my Father, you know everything, so you know how blank I am right now. I turn to you to guide my thoughts today. I have planned, studied and worked as much as I can, and I am still in the dark as to what I should do. Help me to relax and open my mind to your supreme understanding, so that I can hear your voice and receive your wisdom. Thank you for showing me how to share my wisdom. I know you will answer, so I praise you now, my omniscient God. Amen.*

# X

## EXCLUSION

The painful truth is that millions of people who are of color, and others considered 'minorities' – even if they aren't – have experienced what it is like to be excluded. This exclusion, being based on other people's prejudices, ignorance and xenophobic machinations, is an evil that has robbed society of the best there could be. Now, lip service is given to diversity to comply with changing laws, rather than to vigorously pursue it. Despite that, we know that within groups who are of the same color, creed, and background, there is also exclusion and discrimination as humans continue to categorize and judge each other.

It was Jesus Christ who started the revolt, activism and social transformation in addition to offering salvation, when He taught that there is no longer Greek or Jew, male or female, when He gave Gentiles authority to be part of God's Kingdom. Don't let any kind of exclusion precipitate fear, dread or depression in you, if you are a Christian. Remember that you are of a chosen priesthood and joint heir with Christ. Maintain your high calling.

## Bible Verse:

Live in harmony with one another. Do not be proud, but be willing to associate with people of low position. Do not be conceited. Do not repay anyone evil for evil. Be careful to do what is right in the eyes of everyone.
**Romans 12:16-18**

## Prayer:

*Lord, you are always watching. You see the situations which bring pain and hurt to everyone who is being robbed, and those being enslaved and trafficked. I ask you to avenge those who are depriving others of their right to freedom and of deserved positions and opportunities to earn a living and provide for their families. Open the eyes of evil doers so that they repent and do right. I pray for myself, my family and communities where people are being deprived by government systems, private industry and individuals in charge. Dear Lord, intervene and enlighten us what to do and how to act. We pray in faith, praising you for your goodness and grace. Amen.*

# eXcess

God does not mind excess. He deals in abundance and overflow. We are the ones putting a negative twist on excessive wealth and special favors from God. God even *threatens* us with 'blessings overtaking us', as shown in the verses below. Excess, however, needs to be taken seriously for other reasons. If we seek to receive more than we deserve, if we cheat others, and if we waste what we have been blessed with, that's excess in the negative.

God's good excess is endless, like all the varieties of nature that God has created for us to enjoy and benefit from. His wonders are without limit – endless universe for us still to investigate and understand, after being on the planet for millennia. God does not tell us to pray for a little of this, and a little of that. He is waiting to pour out from the windows of heaven on us. Sometimes that's too scary for us to grasp, because we have become so accustomed to less.

When you scream and shout your praises, scream for more. God abundantly pardons, as well as abundantly blesses. Why don't we test Him and see what happens?

## Bible Verse:

If you fully obey the LORD your God and carefully follow all his commands I give you today, the LORD your God will set you high above all the nations on earth. All these blessings will come on you and accompany you if you obey the LORD your God: You will be blessed in the city and blessed in the country. The fruit of your womb will be blessed, ... **Deuteronomy 28:1-4**

## Prayer:

*Lord, consume me with your abundance. Let me think abundance every day that I awake. If I always have enough of your goodness, I have more to share. Lord, open all our eyes to see how much of your abundance we have. You are in the invisible, the intangible as well as the material things. Thank you for keeping us safe when we travel by air, land or sea; for keeping us safe from the upsets in nature. Thank you for strangers who help us when we are in difficulty; for creating our family members for us to love and to make our lives meaningful. Abundant God, we worship and praise you for all overflow, as we believe. Precious Jesus. Amen and Amen.*

# Y

## YES

'Yes' represents surrender, among other things. We are called to say 'YES' in obedience to the call of God on our lives. We learn to say 'no' very early in our lives, yet we fail to use it later when we really need to say a loud 'NO'. No was an exercise of power of choice and independence of thought, once we began to use language. As adults, we need to learn to say 'YES' to what is positive and 'NO' to what is negative, both for us individually and to others with whom we are in contact.

Sometimes we don't say 'yes' because we are afraid of being overwhelmed by the scope of some opportunity or offer in our life or we might be feeling 'unprepared'. However, it would be very wise to weigh all sides of any decision affecting our present or our future, before rushing to agree to what we may live to regret. Make a list of how many times you have said 'no' when you should have said 'yes' or vice versa. Often our 'yes' is silent when we allow the wrong things to go on, without standing up for what's right.

# Bible Verse:

Let no one deceive you with empty words..... Have nothing to do with the fruitless deeds of darkness, but rather expose them.... Be very careful, then, how you live – not as unwise but as wise, making the most of every opportunity, because the days are evil.
**Ephesians 5: 6,11,15**

# Prayer:

*Lord and Master, to whom I now say 'yes'. Yes, Lord, yes. I want to serve you. I have been negligent in doing your will. Please forgive me. What greater work can I do but be surrendered to your will and leading. I pray for your power to discern what is right and holy for me to choose and what will bring me 'good success'. I want to say 'yes' only to what is of good report both in my thoughts and in my actions. I surrender to your powerful purpose in my life and wait to follow the insights from your Holy Spirit. In Jesus's great and healing name, Amen.*

# YESTERDAY

There are many yesterday experiences that we shudder to think of and wish that they never occurred.  People stand judgment today for what they did in their yesterdays and people also go insane thinking about what they did yesterday. Even generations of people are suffering for the sins of their parents in past decades. Yesterday's toll cannot be ignored. Reaping and sowing go together, as we know.

What are we doing to make sure that what we do today does not create a yesterday that will be hard to live down? Thank God, however, that we can move on from our yesterdays, once God's hand has touched us and remolded us into His image. Save your energy and do not be weighed down by your past.

## Bible Verse:

If we claim to be without sin, we deceive ourselves and the truth is not in us. If we confess our sins, he is faithful and just and will forgive us our sins and purify us from all unrighteousness. If we claim we have not sinned, we make him out to be a liar and his word is not in us.
**1 John 1:8-10**


## Prayer:

*Divine and Holy God, in Heaven, please hear my prayer today as I ask you to unburden me of yesterday, with its pains and hurts and mistakes. I know that you do not see us, but Jesus and His shed blood. However, being human, I sometimes have my memory interrupting my thoughts. I want to live in the present and rely on the power of the Holy Spirit in my life, so I ask for your help in freeing my mind and my focus. Lord, I want to be ready to receive the power from on high without any blockage. I give you my yesterday today and praise you for a future that I know will overflow with your grace, blessings and mercy. In the mighty and powerful name of Jesus, I pray. Amen.*

# Z

## ZENITH

Those who climb mountains usually hope to reach the peak and are driven in their desire to conquer the heights and get there. Those who race cars and horses and anything else that involves speed hope to be first, to break records and to do better than they ever did before or better than anyone else before them. That is aiming for the zenith. The zenith is north of any level where you may be now or where you have ever been. The zenith takes courage, practice, planning and endurance. Not everyone sets themselves a zenith. Many are o.k. with watching others climb, or with cheering on others who win.

Is there a zenith of which you have stopped short? That is often the case – stopping just before you get there. The sad thing is that you don't know that. It feels like you will never make it and that is why you stop. Now, go for it! It's in the celestial sphere. There is no limit to your reach or resources. Never doubt that.

## Bible Verse:

I can do all things through him who strengthens me.
**Philippians 4:13**

## Prayer:

*Almighty, redeeming God, I have stayed in the shadow too long. I have not used all the gifts that you have given me. I have not shared all the graces with which I am blessed, so that others will experience you through what I share. Holy, holy God, forgive me for this and let me aim for more **You** to shine through me. Let me draw on your wisdom, your love and your energy to bless those around me. You are my rock and I depend on you, as I humbly pray in Jesus's name. Amen.*

# ZEITGEIST

This is German, which I speak, and it refers to the 'spirit of the time'. English has decided to borrow the term. It references whatever is the predominant frame of mind and preoccupation of a generation or an era. We know for sure that the domination of other races was the preoccupation of European colonists, and the remnants of that age are left over today. Zeitgeist is the background determining what people are willing to accept as normal, acceptable or desirable.

I don't have to itemize all the alarming things that are now seen as commonplace and open for the taking, in this century, which would have had people ostracized, imprisoned or exiled in the past. The spirit of the time has changed and will continue to change. Despite that, there are those values, universal wisdom, purpose and spiritual directives which must remain the same – Zeitgeist or no Zeitgeist. The spirit we follow, most safely, is the Holy Spirit within us.

## Bible Verse:

Now Stephen, a man full of God's grace and power, performed great wonders and signs among the people. Opposition arose, however, from members of the Synagogue of the Freedmen (as it was called)—Jews of Cyrene and Alexandria as well as the provinces of Cilicia and Asia—who began to argue with Stephen. But they could not stand up against the wisdom the Spirit gave him as he spoke. Then they secretly persuaded some men to say, "We have heard Stephen speak blasphemous words against Moses and against God."
**Acts 6:8-11**

## Prayer:

*Dear Loving God who has stood with me and in whom I live and move and have my being, even when I was not conscious of that, I pray to you now to open my eyes and let me see the truth about all my situations. Let me rest in your love and be wise to what you are showing me. Help me to live by revelation and not by circumstances. Let your divine Spirit pervade all my thoughts and words so that I live only in and through your power.*

*I ask you to rescue me from myself, from my environment and from any thought trying to invade my mind and lead me away from you and the blessings you have for me. I want to stay within your will so that what I do will only glorify you. I pray this prayer for every day of life going forward and thank you right now for the answers. In your mighty name I pray. Amen.*

# AFTERWORD

I appreciate your securing a copy of my book of prayer and inspiration thoughts. I trust that if you have never been a fan of the Bible or an enthusiast for prayer, you will now begin to become one or both. Divert some of that secular energy to spiritual pursuits – shout and jump about what's valuable.

For those who are Christians, but have faltered along the way, not delving into the Word often enough and not praying regularly about everything, I hope that this will trigger an eagerness to get busy letting the Bible speak to you, and busy speaking to God each day.

For those who are weary and even thinking of giving up, I trust that you are re-energized to connect more closely with God, and to no longer doubt Him.

Please check online and at your nearest book store and see the next book with my name as Author. I would appreciate your being part of my regular reading audience, as well as your feedback on what has blessed you: *coachingretreat@gmail.com*.

I trust that you will pray for me.  In Jesus's mighty name, I share His messages.

*Hyacinth E. Gooden-Bailey*

# THE AUTHOR

**Hyacinth Gooden-Bailey** worships at the United Methodist Church in Queens, New York. She is the mother of 4 wonderful children and two grandchildren. She has served the world, planning and coordinating international conferences, on different continents, dealing with the most serious global concerns. Her first career was teaching foreign languages in Kingston, Jamaica, being literate in Spanish, French and German, and training teachers. She is a two-time graduate of the University of the West Indies, Mona, and of New York University, where she received her Master's Degree in Organizational Psychology.  She writes inspirational articles, poetry, short stories and books related to personal transformation and professional development.

Ms. Gooden-Bailey is available for private Life and Career Coaching, especially for women at midlife and beyond, and for group coaching for associations, organizations and teams. She facilitates workshops, tele-classes and retreats. The author invites feedback on how this book has helped you, or someone else, to whom you gave this book as a gift.

Hyacinth E. Gooden-Bailey, M.A., Global Life Transition Coach/Career Change Strategist/Inspirational Speaker and Workshop/Retreat Facilitator

**www.sapiencecoaching.com**

**coachmenow@sapiencecoaching.com**

**https://www.facebook.com/CoachingParExcellence**

**Dear Reader, please check your favorite bookstores and Amazon.com for other inspirational books by the same author, for your spiritual growth, and personal and professional development**

**Author:**

**Hyacinth E. Gooden-Bailey, M.A.**

Made in the USA
Columbia, SC
13 January 2018